VISION, CLARITY, SUPPORT

A LEADERSHIP CRASH COURSE ON THE 3 PILLARS OF SUCCESS

LORENZO FLORES

Mangrove Publishing

VISION, CLARITY, SUPPORT

A LEADERSHIP CRASH COURSE ON THE 3 PILLARS OF SUCCESS

FOREWORD

It is often said that a career in retail finds you and not the other way around. I started my retail journey 30 years ago thinking it would be a short-lived step to something else. As a part-time store employee I quickly realized that I loved the day-to-day interaction with employees and customers, and I could not imagine myself doing anything else. Today I absolutely believe one of the very best experiences for teaching someone to be a great leader is running a store. I learned more about leadership in my 10+ years as Store Leader than in any other role. The role of a Store Leader provides the unique vantage point of seeing the inter-dependencies of all functional areas of the business—merchandising, marketing, supply chain, finance, etc.— come together to, ultimately, create both the employee and customer experience. In other words, the Store Leader role drives systemic thinking. Finally, Store Leaders understand that leadership is about working in the grey. Leadership is not linear and there is not a perfect one-size-fits-all solution to every problem. In any given day a Store Leader is presented with situations and problems that cannot be planned for in advance. They use the values system of the organization as a set of guiding principles in problem solving versus following a set of policies and procedures.

Over my career I have learned there are three core competencies that distinguish good leaders from great leaders. First, great leaders hire great people and build high performance teams. And in order to build high performance teams you must first build trusting relationships, have the ability to communicate the "why" for everything the team sets out to do and provide clarity around goals and objectives. Second, great leaders provide their teams a high level of psychological safety. This means creating an environment where people feel comfortable taking risks, making mistakes, sharing concerns openly and bringing their best selves to work. Finally, great leaders are great storytellers. Storytellers provide context and real-life examples that deeply connect, engage and inspire the team.

I met Lorenzo 15 years ago when I was the Store Leader at the Best Buy store in Westminster, California. I quickly realized Lorenzo embodies all three of these core competencies. Lorenzo understands that leadership is about the ability to influence and inspire others and not about a title. While I did not know what specific leadership role he would have on my team, what I did know was that he was someone I absolutely needed to help lead the change in the endeavor ahead of us.

Many leadership books teach through theory and process instead of context grounded in real life experiences. I am grateful Lorenzo is choosing to share his leadership philosophy with us through the lens of his real life leadership journey. And, yes, Lorenzo is a great storyteller! What makes this book compelling is that he is sharing all of his learnings from the vantage point of the Store Leader role. People who know me well often hear me say that the Store Leader is one of, if not, *the* most important roles in any retail organization. We rely on them to inspire and engage the majority of the organization's workforce.

This book will help leaders create a vision that connects uniquely with everyone on a team, clearly define expectations of the team (while also clearly defining what the team can expect from the leader) and, finally, how the leader can effectively support the team in a way that drives a high performing, highly engaged organization.

- Gil Dennis

Gil Dennis has spent his entire 30 year career in retail. He is currently the Executive Vice President of Retail, Human Resources and Customer Experience for Indigo. Prior to working at Indigo, Gil was the Senior Vice President of Stores at dressbarn, a division of Ascena Retail Group. Prior to dressbarn, Gil worked at Best Buy for 10 years in various Retail and Human Resources leadership roles.

INTRODUCTION

Vision, Clarity, Support: A Leadership Crash Course on the 3 Pillars of Success is your next stepping stone to accelerating your own leadership capabilities, opening communication through connection, and improving employee efficiency in today's workplace. It is intended to be a short reference guide, ready to be implemented immediately. Other leadership theory and quick-fix books miss out on meeting leaders where they currently stand. This book recognizes there are a range of leaders, from those with significant tenure to those who are brand new to the role to those who've yet to earn the title but feel the drive to contribute to their team today. We know you're ready to make changes, and the tools provided within this book are designed in a way to fit every level of leadership. It will lend real-life examples to relate to the current state of your business and provide the steps necessary to create a lasting impact on your leaders, your employees, and the community.

MY PROMISE TO YOU:

Rather than throw concrete solutions at you, I will supply the questions necessary to lead you to the unique solutions that will work best for your team. Instead of focusing on theory, I will provide actions you can take right now, before you even finish reading. This is the book to read, set aside, and reference often. It should be covered in pencil marks and highlighter, and the page corners should be dog-eared.

What you won't get is corporate talk, cheesy acronyms to memorize, or a one-size-fits-all approach. Let's face it, our experiences are rarely "one-sized".

What you will get is an in-depth look at the three themes that will set you up for success: Vision, Clarity, and Support.

- Why they're important
- What they mean to you and your job
- What "great" looks like
- How you can do it
- How to tell if they're working

We'll discuss how the three work together and what can be accomplished when they align, and you'll be able to take practical steps throughout to evaluate how close you are to bringing these three pillars into your workplace. I'd place a bet right now that you're closer than you think, and many of the elements described in the pages that follow will seem familiar. It's just a matter of taking care to ensure each pillar is given its own attention. Let's take what's already working for you and make it even better.

By understanding, embracing, and utilizing my 3 Pillars of Success, any leader of people will improve their ability to connect with their teams in a way that creates trust, loyalty and empowerment, ultimately leading to a work environment that emanates credibility, productivity, and ongoing success.

WHO SHOULD READ THIS BOOK?

Vision, Clarity, Support: A Leadership Crash Course on the—you know what? Let's just refer to it as *The 3 Pillars* from here on out.

The 3 Pillars caters to a wide audience that includes leaders, aspiring leaders, and the entire generation of workforce employees who were born in the age of technology. Philosophies are shifting, career expectations are expanding, and the ways of leading in generations past are no longer capable of keeping up with the workforce of today.

The 3 Pillars is meant to inspire and open a conversation amongst those who want to lead well and those who want to be led well. You may find yourself in one of these categories:

THE LEADERS: This book is a tool to aid you in self-reflection. This may be your first time hearing about The 3 Pillars: Vision, Clarity, and Support, but these theories are naturally occurring. In a workplace that seems to be well-aligned, with a cohesive team and happy customers, The 3 Pillars are most likely already in effect. If this is the case, this book will help you understand why the well-oiled machine is working so efficiently and where to go from here. If this doesn't describe your current work environment, now is the time to make changes and bring on great success! In the pages that follow, you'll be encouraged to consider the feedback you've received from employees and peers. This is merely the kindling; you'll be the spark that ignites a path to constructive conversations and empowerment. *The 3 Pillars* will help you define roles, lay out clear expectations, and eliminate miscommunication. You'll be left with a new perspective that will advance you as a leader. You'll uncover opportunities that are ready for action right now, and you'll transform day-to-day reactionary behavior into proactive teamwork.

THE CONTRIBUTORS: You may not be a leader yet, but perhaps you aspire to be. Or maybe you're satisfied where you are but want to take on a more proactive role in improving your workplace. After all, this is your life, and if you can better it, why not? This book will provide insight on what it's like to be a part of leadership in a company—what it's like to make difficult decisions, prioritize time and handle problems that may have conflicting solutions. After reading this, you can evaluate and reset your own expectations. You'll recognize the dynamics of leadership within your own work environment. Better yet, you'll uncover ways in which you can challenge your leaders to be even better. Perhaps your environment isn't as productive or inspired as you'd like. A mentor once told me, *"You deserve the leadership you tolerate."* Are you satisfied with how things currently stand at your job? Do you want them to be better? Do you want to love going into work each day? Do you want to be surrounded by those who inspire and support you? You can do something about it!

Whether your title states it or not, you're reading this because you serve the role of a leader. *The 3 Pillars* is the resource you need to ensure positive growth, maximum success and, ultimately, team satisfaction.

This is the book for leaders, by a leader.

Understanding
Those We Lead

I grew up in Michigan amongst all the car manufacturing plants. They had a magic weapon that allowed for things like brand new cars and credit cards: the workers' unions. The unions empowered employees and prevented them from being treated as disposable. They aided them in finding new jobs and opportunities, and things like overtime could be treated as guaranteed salary. It was a time of excess.

I was in middle school when they shut down Willow Run Plant and watched as friends and family were impacted by its closure.

Suddenly, there were mass lay-offs and lost pensions. Where people once spent decades working for the same company, now they were no longer taken care of by those businesses. The valuable, hard-earned skills these employees had developed were nontransferable, and they couldn't find new jobs easily. They lost their livelihood when their once stable industry became unreliable.

The children of these unfortunate employees witnessed the developing distrust that ensued and quickly learned a new philosophy on life—one grounded in purpose and happiness rather than things and stuff. This new generation started considering what they wanted in life, and then strived to build a career path that would get it. Jobs weren't just for paying the bills anymore. Employees wanted fun; they wanted to find what they loved and make money doing it. Creativity, passion, and satisfaction replaced the previous priorities of big homes, nice cars and affluence.

We've all possessed these sorts of dreams, but the new generation had something previous generations never did: an explosion of technology. With access to the entire world, we were all able to watch as people made their wildest dreams come true. The internet provided new resources: social media, digital storefronts and countless ways to share. Today, entrepreneurialism is possible for anyone with a vision and the drive to act on it. People can make careers for themselves. They can be influencers. And it's this mindset that leaves so much room for growth, self-satisfaction, and opportunity to impact those around us.

However...

This leads to a huge disconnect between the leaders of previous generations and today's workforce. There are new expectations and standards, and you can quickly be left behind if you don't understand modern technology, the purpose of social media, concepts like Kickstarter, and even how to find information through today's most relevant news sources. I've heard leaders say things like, "Oh, I don't use social media." They wear it like it's simply something they aren't into, but this is today's method of communication. There's so much happening that when you aren't in tune with where we're going socially, where our employees are gathering their information and how this content shapes opinions, then you aren't connected. If your focus as a leader is simply on business results, you're going to be seen as someone who doesn't relate, doesn't understand and, at worst, doesn't care.

Today's workforce is brilliant. They're fearless and can do things in an instant that once took so much time and effort. I was a latchkey kid responsible for my sister, and my mom would call every day on her lunch break, 12:15, with things for us to do and lessons to learn. There used to be infomercials for encyclopedia sets, the valuable reference tool you could have in your own home? We had a set of those, and we'd have to use them to look up topics and write reports. It took time and effort to seek this knowledge. We had to work to learn, using these massive references or seeking information from those with the knowledge. Access to information was barely there.

Now it's instant. We can immediately find answers and instantly express our opinions. I can ask a question and have an answer from a credible source in less than five minutes. This makes retention of the information unnecessary, as well, as it takes little effort to re-retrieve it. Need to fix your sink? Google it. You can be your own handyman with a couple videos. Car making a strange noise? Compare it to other uploaded audio files and find out the exact problem. Because of the internet, we can learn constantly, and this generation has grown up with that.

This immediate gratification and access has consequences though. Committing to something that takes awhile can be a struggle when everything else is nearly effortless to attain. Because of this, it's important for leaders to take the time to understand each employee on a deeper level. What do they hope to achieve? How can we guide them?

We want them to chase their dreams.

That may seem counterintuitive to the success of our business, but it's true. Just as quickly as we can learn how to repave our backyard patio, we can access the success stories of those who've started new businesses, carved out their own niche in an industry or made careers out of consulting. There are so many examples of these people who've proven you can go after what you want and attain massive success. This generation has a built-in entrepreneurial spirit, and if they feel like what they're doing today isn't helping them get to their goals, then you'll lose them. They won't show up with their best, if they even show up at all.

PART I: VISION

WHY IT'S IMPORTANT (OR, *WHY:* IT'S IMPORTANT)

"Back to the Basics"

"Buy-In"

"Re-Engage"

"WIIFM [What's In It For Me?]"

Over the life of my retail career, I've heard these terms so often they've lost their meaning. Outdated, cliché, these do nothing more than speak to a lack of true vision. Sure, they sound catchy and could be printed on a poster for the break room walls, but at the end of the day, people want to know why they need to do things: why they should interact with customers a certain way, why they should communicate more openly with their coworkers, why they should feel energized—not aggravated—about Sunday morning meetings.

And you know what? They *deserve* a why.

If I asked you right now to take a dollar bill, drive to the gas station, and put it on the counter in front of the cashier, I'd be willing to bet your first question, naturally, would be, "Why?"

Now, imagine I told you she's the luckiest cashier in the world, and your odds of buying a winning lottery ticket off of her are extremely favorable. For most people, their motivation and interest in taking my advice will be much greater once this *why* is known.

Similarly, if we're trying to convince our teams to do specific tasks or refresh themselves on selling strategies or operational processes, connecting them to the *why* is the first step to getting them to follow through. It creates a sense of focus, demonstrates respect, and presents the team with a unified goal.

Your Vision is your why.

THE SMALL PICTURE IS THE BIG PICTURE.

Sometimes a company vision is grandiose and noble. In these instances, the *why* may be "To make the world a better place." Here are three examples of how big, broad visions lead directly to big, broad actions:

VISION BASED ON:	LEADS TO ACTIONS, SUCH AS:
Community	Providing community services or creating a great product that benefits all
Charity	Donating percentages of profits to help others throughout the world
Environment	Promoting a sustainable Earth and utilizing green initiatives

More often, however, vision is much more specific to the job or industry, yet the reasoning behind it is just as important as any worldly goal. Additionally, a broad vision can be fine-tuned or broken down into smaller pieces—sorting out the elements retail leaders deal with every day.

Consider sales results and how they determine payroll. More hours equals more people working, equals more leaders needed, equals more promotions available. A vision directly influences this domino effect of growth. How's that? Ask yourself these questions:

Do you know what goals your team must achieve and maintain to increase payroll?

If so, *does your team know?*

Do they understand how a daily sales goal (or a units per transaction goal) can build more opportunities for full-time positions, providing more help on the sales floor?

Bringing the entire team into the vision not only helps them understand the *why*, it gives them incentive to work toward goals that benefit them individually and help the company as a whole. A team that understands the vision won't be working merely to avoid having to attend performance calls or writing action plans. They'll strive to achieve the goals that increase their opportunities for promotion, for full-time hours, and for more support.

Exceeding goals to increase opportunity is a simple vision that can lead to exceptional results. It may not be "saving the world", but it's the type of vision we want to create and implement as leaders.

WRONG VISIONS AND HOW TO AVOID THEM

Not all visions are created equally, and supporting the wrong one can lead to inconsistent results, employee frustration, and high turnover. It's not always easy to identify a wrong vision, either, especially if we've been trained to follow a vision that's been taught to us.

Have you ever noticed an employee who tends to stay in the middle of the pack? You know the one—they don't want to be in the spotlight, but they manage to stay out of the bottom. If they do just enough to be slightly better than some of their peers, they won't have to deal with much attention from the boss or corporate. Turns out, this, too, is a vision—*stay in the middle and be left alone*, and it occurs throughout the hierarchy of a company, from entry-level associates to store managers and beyond. This lazy vision is one many retail leaders have perpetuated, and—you guessed it—it's wrong.

In order to avoid wrong visions, we return, once again, to the *why*. What is the end goal of the vision? To be left alone by the higher ups? Not only does this wrong vision reinforce a negative mindset, it offers nothing that can benefit the employee or the company. If the vision and the reasons behind it are vague, pessimistic, or simply a concept that was engrained into our heads over the years by somebody else, it's time to reexamine and revise.

WHY YOU SHOULD CARE

As a leader, particularly as a leader reading this book, you want to achieve and exceed your goals. There's no doubt in my mind this is true. We all want top performing teams, and now we simply need to make sure they know it—and they know why.

A vision that focuses on employee development and product knowledge would see a sustainable lift in results. Measuring success based on internal promotions and opportunities would encourage your team to push harder, knowing they're responsible for their own accomplishments. These focused, specific visions are the ones that'll glean direct results. You'll find yourself proudly sharing the work your team has done—the improvements they've made—and consequently, will inspire other leaders to do the same with their teams.

So why should we care about vision? The answer is simple. A team *without* a vision will inevitably create its own, and there's no guarantee it will align with your company's expectations. They may settle for that middle ground approach to be left alone, or they may fall back on the short-sighted "What's in it for me?" concept, creating a personal vision that only focuses on benefitting them. No matter, a lack of vision puts us, and our teams, at risk. We must create consistency, opportunities, and results, by implementing a team-wide vision. After all, we're leaders, and it's up to us to guide the team to success.

FORGET WHY. *WHAT* IS A VISION?

Okay, you get it. Having a clear and concise vision is important. Employees deserve to know why they should do the things they're asked. It benefits everyone.

But what exactly is a vision?

Here's the simple explanation: A vision defines the values of a team or a company, and it helps to guide proper behaviors.

Of course, you know by now I'm not just going to stop there. Let's look at it more in depth.

In the retail world, we see visions as credos, mission statements, company values, manifestos, et cetera. You've seen it before. You've probably memorized it, too (bonus points if it's part of your email signature). The challenge, though, is we're expected to take these flowery, inspirational words and bring them to life within our teams. We must demonstrate the concept, making it a part of our everyday language. It's easier said than done, right?

A consumer just threw a product across the cash wrap, spitting out obscenities that make us want to wash our hands. How is the poster hanging in our office—the one reminding us about the "world class" customer service we're required to provide—going to help in this scenario?

Okay, this is a more extreme example but we, as leaders, are expected to maintain our composure, modeling what we expect of our teams when they're in similar situations.

The poster in our office is a corporate vision. It's meant to create alignment and set standards of excellence with a clear direction and purpose. As leaders, we're responsible for passing down this vision to our employees. Memorizing a quote won't do us any good. The last thing we want to do is parrot well-intentioned phrases over and over.

What we can do is set the example and clearly communicate with our team.

They look to us for guidance in the most challenging situations. What we need to accomplish is connecting the dots between what corporate expects and how it comes to life in our stores.

HOW DO WE CREATE OUR VISION?

Our company has provided us with standards, inspiration, and encouragement. Now's the time to take these elements and add our personal flair. Inspect the company vision, and see where it relates directly to our stores and our teams. This will help everyone feel the mission is more local and relevant. There's no need to create a vision from scratch, either. In fact, it's important to remember people leave *managers,* not companies, and often the dissatisfaction from an employee is a result of the inconsistency between the company vision and the manager's vision. Just as we want our employees' individual goals to align with our store's, our vision must align with the company's.

Consider the unique qualities and needs of your store. How can you transform the company's mission statement or credo into a clear, concise vision that can be brought to life daily?

Perhaps your company...

Is committed to diversity and employee empowerment.

Strives to make sure everyone is heard.

Encourages the team to challenge each other in the right ways.

Includes the team in decisions and strategies.

How do we, in our stores, make sure these ideals are a reality—every day?

If our vision involves encouraging our team to challenge each other, then we create avenues to make sure this happens. This sets the foundation to build a more efficient, competent team and gives them the control to help their peers grow. These are actionable measures that stem from the company-wide vision, and they'll benefit both the store and the individual employee.

WE AREN'T THE ONLY ONES.

The individuals on our team each have their own personal vision or motivation for working: income to pay the bills, career advancement, opportunities to learn, tuition reimbursement, health benefits, bonuses.

It's important to understand each employee's goals and tie them to our vision. If they can attach their personal or professional goals to the behaviors we want to happen every day, they'll see the benefit in executing the vision.

AN EXAMPLE...

Courtney is a part-time cashier. She wants to make more money but, being a full-time student, she can only work nights and weekends. Her income pays for a car loan, but she'd really like to save extra money for a Spring Break trip abroad next year. Her goal is to make more by joining the sales team, but working at the register limits her opportunities to demonstrate her selling skills.

Our company's mission statement says, "Value your people and reward them for their unique contributions." It also says, "Develop talent and offer learning experiences." It's time to make these visions actionable.

How can we offer her a learning experience that will also benefit the store's results?

How can we develop her selling skills while she's working as a cashier?

Most importantly, how can we take her personal vision—to make more money for the trip abroad—and align it with our company's vision?

Here's the chance to bring a mission statement to life.

SHARE THE WEALTH (OF KNOWLEDGE).

We've got our vision. Now, it's time to turn it into part of our team's culture.

First, how do we make sure *we're* following our vision? We know what we want to accomplish, but without external insight, we may be missing important opportunities as leaders. We need to be brutally honest with ourselves and our team can help with that.

<u>**To start, follow these steps:**</u>

1) Take a few minutes to write down three things you stand for as a leader. This is your personal leadership vision.

2) Select a diverse sample of your employees and ask them to, individually, write down three things that they feel define your leadership vision.

3) Compare their answers to yours. Are they identical? Are they completely different?

4) Answer these: Do you see elements of the company vision in your personal leadership vision? Did your team recognize these elements in how you lead?

5) Consider creating a strategy (SMART goals, SWOT analysis, business reviews, strategy plans) to better develop and demonstrate your leadership vision.

Next, after we evaluate our vision, we must find ways to share and reinforce it. We can start by mentioning it during every meeting and every conversation we have with our team. Again, we're not parrots. Don't just repeat a phrase that's been fine-tuned. Relate it to current behaviors, trends, or needs of the store. Attach it to tangible examples so the team can better understand ways to bring it to life.

When we notice a team member executing the vision, provide them with in-the-moment positive recognition. On the other hand, when we're falling behind on goals or objectives, try to identify behaviors that aren't aligning with the vision and provide timely, specific feedback when wrong behaviors are witnessed.

Making sure everyone is familiar with the vision and providing real-time feedback are the most direct actions we can take to reinforce the vision.

WHEN DO WE KNOW THEY'VE REALLY CAUGHT ON?

Verifying whether or not the team has an aligned vision is as simple as asking, "What is our vision?" If they can't answer quickly and confidently, there's still work to do. The more we reiterate it, the more comfortable everyone will become explaining what it is and what it means to them.

Seek out behaviors for validation. I've found that teams with aligned visions:

- Include team leaders that can make unified decisions about customer service or employee issues faster
- Have less concerns from their employees about their career paths and personal development
- See an increase in specific customer compliments, many mentioning an employee by name
- Share everyday language that is reflective of the company vision

THE NEXT STEPS

The duty of maintaining a vision within a retail environment is ongoing. Challenges of leadership turnover, new hires, performance expectations, and seasonal priorities require that we keep our teams motivated and energized, while making sure everyone is up-to-date on our standards and expectations. In order to incubate an environment of consistency, inspiration, and development, we must strive to teach and reinforce our vision, handle issues by providing real-time feedback, and praise all of our team members when we witness them demonstrating exemplary behavior. Leaders bring the vision to life by weaving it into everyday language and actions, and in return, promote workplaces that strive to benefit both the company *and* the employee.

A STORY ABOUT VISION

John is a part-time employee who left his previous job in search of more opportunity. He likes our company and has a passion for what we sell. John's personal goal, his vision, is to gain a full-time position in order to receive benefits and have a consistent paycheck.

A customer approaches me about an issue after having talked to John first. Turns out, we're sold out of a product he wants.

"What were you looking to buy?" I ask. "Is there a reason you need it today?"

He tells me, "I don't, but I've been watching the price for the past few months, and I'd like to get it while it's on sale."

I offer to help him order it online, having it shipped to his home. He's happy with this simple resolution, but asks, "Why didn't John give me the same option?"

The customer has a point, so later, when the traffic's decreased and John has a spare moment, I pull him aside. After retelling my interaction with an anonymous customer who was upset we didn't have a product in stock, I ask John, "How would you react in this situation?"

John looks around for a second before answering. "I'd apologize and suggest an alternate item."

"That's a potential option, sure, but what if we dug deeper and found he didn't need the product today?"

I barely finish my question when John answers, "We could order it for him online."

I nod my head and tell him that's the exact same resolution we came to. It ensured the customer got what he wanted and he left happy.

Next, I follow up with another question. "What's our company's vision?"

John says, "To create great customer experiences that result in loyalty and ownership," and he's exactly right.

"What's our store vision?" I ask. Remember, we want all of our employees to answer this quickly and confidently. This is the vision I've created to be unique to my team while aligning to the company's expectations.

John smiles. "That, as long as the customer walks out of here thinking we're awesome and that they've had a great experience, then we're happy."

He's got the company and store vision down. That leaves one other. "What's your personal vision when it comes to customers?"

"Pretty much the same as the store's. I think about it as if they're my family, and how I'd want to treat them."

I commend him on his vision but ask, "If a customer comes in looking for an item we're sold out of, what should your response be?"

"I'd ask more questions, like, if they need it today, so I can help them get what they're looking for." Then he pauses for a second. "I had a customer this morning... Was that the guy you helped?"

I admit it was but tell John this has been an excellent opportunity for us to discuss our vision and how we can bring it to life in the store. Going forward, he can share this story with others, encouraging his coworkers, and sharing his personal vision, thus working on his own growth and development.

Ensuring his vision aligned with the rest of the store not only improved his customer interactions, it led him to the full-time position he wanted and eventually a promotion into leadership. Feeling more motivated and inspiring others, John and his team have performed consistently and have been recognized for their outstanding customer service.

This is the power of a clearly-defined vision.

PART II: CLARITY

Samuel works in the tech department of a popular retail store. He's been there for almost a year, provides exemplary customer support, and stays up-to-date on changing technologies. It's not hard to imagine he'll move into a leadership role himself, eventually.

One day, his manager, Tony, walks by, stops at an endcap, and asks Samuel, "Hey, can you clean this up? Make it more presentable?"

He then walks to the back of the store to work on his next task. Samuel considers the placement of the endcap, recognizing how visible it is from the entrance doors, and gets to work. He pulls all the product from the shelves, cleans everything, relocates items that never seem to sell, and sets it all back up. The endcap is now clean, organized, and appealing to anyone who walks by.

Tony comes by later and stops again. He looks the shelves up and down and says, "Thanks, but this isn't what I had in mind."

Turns out, Tony wants a new product brand to be the focus of that space, and he wants more peripherals on display to complement the brand and encourage those sales. None of this was made evident to Samuel, who hides his discouragement as he begins the task again.

In this situation, we've had a serious breakdown in Clarity.

EXPECTATIONS ALL AROUND

We've created our vision, but that's only the beginning. In order to implement it and make sure everyone's actions align to it, we must be extremely clear with our expectations. It's easy to say we'll clarify the employee's role: reviewing the job description, having them repeat it back to us, and, of course, they need to know what they can and cannot do; however, clarity is a two-way street. We must not only be clear about what's expected of our employees. We must also be sure they fully understand what to expect from us as leaders. This second half is equally vital.

Let's take this a step further. Don't just tell them what they can expect from you, tell them how you plan to help them. Ask them, "What do you expect from me so that you can best do your job and feel supported in your role?"

This step isn't only necessary at the beginning of their job. It's a question to follow-up on during each performance review.

How can leadership help you improve in your role?

What can leadership do to help you remain successful?

If you find yourself having to review job descriptions on occasion, add in, "What do you need from leadership to avoid these conversations?"

Essentially, clarity in the workplace is taking the time to sit down with people, ask what they're trying to accomplish, provide them with clear explanations of what's expected of them, and extend the conversation to discovering what they expect from us as leaders. The open communication and equal understanding for what we're all trying to achieve promotes a great work environment filled with passionate, positive people while ensuring this crucial pillar is spread to all levels of the workplace.

GREAT MINDS DON'T ALWAYS THINK ALIKE.

If we lose focus at this second pillar and aren't clear about expectations, employees will do what they think is right. Step into their shoes for a moment. There's nothing more frustrating than working hard, putting in your full effort, and thinking you're doing the right thing only to be pulled aside and told you aren't. The blame falls on you, the one who did something incorrectly, but it's not your fault if you weren't shown or told the correct process or behaviors.

"I tried hard today. I worked hard. Then they told me it was all wrong."

We can prevent these occurrences by actively investing in what our employees do. Otherwise, we're guaranteed to hit these roadblocks. Rather than having to backtrack and clean up after the miscommunication, we can invest early in assuring clarity is established.

GET SPECIFIC!

Bill was an audio supervisor at Best Buy, and I worked part-time in his department. He had a very clear vision for his department. Cleanliness, organization, and a visually pleasing work environment were key to ensuring customers took us seriously. From day one, he walked me through the expectations of how the department should look at all times. Sales goals were important, of course, but so was dusting. Bill physically demonstrated every aspect of his cleaning expectations, teaching me a routine that assured every inch was cleaned every day. Over the course of a week, the entire department would be scrubbed and spotless. Any time we were slow, we were expected to be cleaning. If we finished the day's cleaning, we were expected to work ahead. Stay ahead of the curve. He was meticulous, maybe even extreme, but he provided clarity by role modeling that exact behavior he wanted. A clean department gave us credibility and it brought to life the idea we were the most knowledgeable, most capable of our field. There was no confusion from me, and because of his practices, it was easy to execute on his vision.

HOW YOU CAN DO IT

WITH NEW HIRES

Conversation. It's that simple, yet, that effective.

During the hiring process, I like to role play the job they're being asked to do. I tell them up front, "If you're going to earn the title, the shirt, the name tag, then you're going to do some improv, right here, right now."

I do this because I not only want to be clear on the expectations, I want to be sure they're comfortable doing the tasks involved in the job title. What I don't want is for their very first experiences in different scenarios to be directly with the customer. Of course, they'll learn from all future customer interactions. They'll continue growing through their job, but there's no need for them to practice their role on an actual customer, not when we have this opportunity to put some common retail occurrences to the test. But there's a catch (spoiler alert).

"I will be the employee. You will be the customer," I tell them.

It immediately throws them off, but how can I expect them to show me what I'm looking for when they've never seen it? And what better way to understand the customer experience than to be in their shoes while learning the expectations of a new job? Here are the steps to my process, and I urge you to try them out yourself:

1) Tell them to "buy" something they actually would be interested in buying. If what your company offers are services, they can inquire about anything that piques their interest. This truly makes them a customer, with real questions, waiting for real answers. This can't be preplanned or scripted by us, and in

this moment we, as leaders, are put on the spot.

2) Leave out some aspects of their training. Don't be the perfect employee who covers every angle. Make the kind of mistakes that should stand out to a new hire who's just learned all the details of the job.

3) Request feedback. They need to learn it's okay to give constructive criticism, even to their leader. I want them to be comfortable telling me what I did wrong. Not only is it acceptable to give feedback, it's expected, and in these role-playing scenarios, we have the perfect opportunity to practice the art of "speaking up".

4) Switch roles. Now your new employee can apply all the elements they just learned through your modeling. As they work through a new scenario, give them time to think through it, encourage

them to ask questions along the way, and collaborate on the ways in which they can best do what's expected.

This role playing prepares the employee before the interactions occur, so consider common challenges faced in your unique workplace and use those to further the training.

With Established Employees

Whether expectations are being met, exceeded, or not, sit down with every member of your store. Set a timer for five minutes and ask them the following:

"What are your next steps in this store?"

Maybe it's a promotion or an experience they want. Maybe their goals extend outside of work—buying a house, buying a car, finishing school, starting school, starting their own business. We want to be aware of these goals.

But that has nothing to do with clarity or employee job expectations!

Oh, but it does. Let me explain.

Employees at most companies have many resources at their disposal—contacts with organizations, access to workshops, internal materials and supportive references—that can help our employees reach their goals. Often, we aren't even aware of these assets, and even when we are, we don't spend time promoting them. After all, we have a day job that fills our schedule plenty. It's worthwhile to dig for them, though, to know what's available. When you meet with your employees, and you learn their aspirations, take notes so you'll understand what it is they want to accomplish professionally and personally. Now, you can share those resources, those opportunities, and show how much more you care about them than numbers and figures.

Furthermore, these conversations—building these connections—helps us to understand our employees' behaviors and attitudes. Knowing where they stand and what they think, we become more aware of how they utilize vision and what they need to grow within the company. We can tailor training methods to their level and assign them responsibilities that we know can challenge them to be better, resulting in greater company efficiency and a more knowledgeable team.

YOU'LL KNOW IT'S WORKING.

When clarity is effectively working, our employees will feel empowered and positive about their role. By demonstrating our passion toward our vision, those we lead will develop a similar passion. Leave out any gray area and our employees will begin coming to us with new ideas. They'll confidently make suggestions and, often, we'll find ourselves quickly incorporating these new ideas into the prior expectations. The hierarchy of the team will blend together. Rather than individual job titles and designated leaders, a "we" will form.

We will follow through on expectations.
We will collaborate to improve the process.
We will succeed.

BONUS

We've put in the effort to build this second pillar tall and strong. The entire workplace appears to be on the same page, and things are running smoothly. Communication is open, everyone is working to achieve the same company vision while also taking advantage of opportunities to fulfill their personal visions.

Let's make things even better.

When we next sit down with our employees, add this question to the conversation:

Do you know anyone personally or professionally who would be a great addition to our organization?

If my employees are doing a fantastic job, then I know they know other fantastic people. It's commonly suggested the five closest people with whom you surround yourself are the ones you're most like. I want to know who those five people are, and if they're interested in endorsing them, they're the first ones I want to apply and bring in for interviews.

Great teams grow great teams.

REVISITING THE BREAKDOWN

Remember Samuel and the breakdown in clarity when his manager, Tony, wanted him to redo the endcap? Samuel put in the effort to do a task well, only to be told it wasn't good enough. Now, he's frustrated, disheartened, and thinking, "Forget it. I'm not going to try anymore."

That one instance may have wasted hours of productive work time, discouraged a valuable employee, and put a dent on future innovation. This is the easiest way to get an employee into the mindset of "They can tell me exactly what they want, and that's what I'll do. Nothing more." Passion is lost and the connection he once had to the job is impacted.

This may be an extreme example of employee disappointment, but the key here is this: Clarity would've prevented it. If clarity exists ahead of time, then we know our employee understands the vision and what's best for the business. Similarly, leadership understands the employee and has worked with them up to this point, focusing on and building their strengths. When given a general task, the employee will feel confident using discretion and taking ownership, even when instructions aren't specific. They can fulfill the task knowing any alterations later are meant to further align to the vision and not to be taken personally. Managers can have confidence in their team to complete jobs, recognizing the steps taken were with their best intentions in mind. Their ability to connect allows the employees to seek them for guidance, as needed, but ultimately, the job done is one that should be productive to the business, fulfill the goals intended, and leave everyone involved feeling it was a job well done.

When someone is new, or is learning something new, it is vital we, as leaders, meet them where they are and provide them with the specifics to do the job well. We can't make assumptions about what they can and cannot do. What we can do, is get on the same page and help move them forward.

Show them.

Demonstrate.

Help them build a level of comfort in their role that ensures we're investing in a team that strives to bring forth the vision.

PART III: SUPPORT

TALK THE TALK. WALK THE WALK.

The workplace now has a sense of belonging and ownership. Employees understand how their behaviors and attitudes drive the bigger business. We've taken the time to dig deeper and recognize personal goals and expectations. Now, it's time to put words into actions. That's where our third pillar—Support—comes into play. Our company vision is established, expectations of employees and leaders are clear, and now we're ready to practice what we've preached.

Providing *support* for them now starts with understanding what support is actually needed. We've taken the time to ask our employees,

"What do you need from us? What do you expect from leadership?" What happens next depends on the individual. It's important to recognize support looks different for different people.

Here's what it's *not*:

- Sending them off blind— A "trial by fire", you could say.
- "They should know what they're doing. If they're any good, they'll figure it out."
- "I think they're smart enough. They've been here long enough, I don't need to spend time teaching them."

Support is not defined by the leader. The idea that support is passed down through legacy and personal feelings is outdated. Let's retire it and provide support based on what is actually needed. Before, those with the most knowledge were the leaders. They often held the highest positions. Modern access to information has changed this dynamic, causing the newer generations in the workforce to need more than knowledge (of which, many will already possess). They need the *why*. They need to feel engaged and understand how their values align to the job at hand.

FAILURE *IS* AN OPTION.

The importance of support is that it encourages people to try, fail, learn, and try again. A prerequisite to leadership is being comfortable in uncomfortable situations. When people are pushing themselves to do things they've never done before—learning new skills, sharpening experiences, working on competencies and strengths—they tend to make mistakes. They may approach something wrong, miss information, or let emotion get in the way. These things naturally happen. Support demonstrates an understanding that it's okay to make these mistakes, as it's how learning takes place. They're more likely to try, take on challenges, pushback, and be receptive to feedback when they know leadership has their backs.

SUPPORT IN ACTION

I recently went for a haircut and shave. After trying a few different barber shops, I've come to have a good sense of those who are professional and worthwhile and those who are still figuring things out. It's good to have options. Since it was last minute, however, I walked in and accepted the first available associate. She sat me down, and we went through the typical barber experience. I've noticed the experienced professionals act similarly, showing off the brand new razor, prepping the hot towel, describing the steps as they do them.

She didn't.

I could tell she was still learning. Meanwhile, in the chair next to mine, I could hear that barber subtly mention things to her.

"Other barbers wring out the towel and check it with the backs of their hands."

She was coaching her, but not in a critical sense. Instead, she was non-confrontational, sharing best practices and tips, and the young woman responded positively.

"I've never thought of that. Thank you."

I could tell this was normal protocol for the woman next to us, as my barber reacted so naturally.

My barber, however, was still uncomfortable. They do neck massages at the end, and as that didn't go so well, either, I wasn't feeling so comfortable myself. Our next-chair barber suggested changing the positioning of my chair. It was tested with enthusiasm, and my barber and I both saw immediate improvement.

The woman next to us could have just as easily ignored the situation, letting my barber figure it out for herself. Instead, she provided in-the-moment support that vastly improved the experience. As the customer, I certainly was grateful.

I share all this because, while it was far from the best shave I've gotten, I decided to email the general manager about my experience. I let them know I appreciated the feeling of their establishment and kindly explained my barber needed a bit more training. She wasn't bad, but for future clients, some improvement would help. Finally, I shared how much I liked the way our next-chair barber provided tips throughout, correcting her in a way that showed excellent leadership and support without making me, as the client, wonder, "What the hell am I doing trusting this person?" It was as simple as that.

Later, I received a phone call from the general manager, who ended up being none other than our next-chair barber.

"You must lead people," she said.

We talked on leadership and support, and she made it very apparent that she's a leader who aims to help her employees. I have no doubts the barber who did my shave has become exceptional in her workplace.

Support can be as simple as reminding a barber to test the temperature of a hot towel. It can be more complex by including role-playing or implementing new training resources. What's important is that it appropriately fits the employee who needs it, encourages growth, and leaves that employee feeling more empowered than they did before.

STAY CONNECTED AND COMMITTED TO GROWTH.

Take a step back and ask, multiple times, what do they need? Break the mold of previous leaders. Many times, the answers will be the same: transparency, honesty, constructive feedback, and accountability. I've found time plays a role, as well. They want time to absorb information and new feedback and work through it down to an emotional level. Then there's the follow-up. They may not request this, but from my experiences—the teams I've helped build—I've seen the greatest success from continuing the conversation.

Where are we with the things we've already discussed?

Is there anything else needed?

Consider their reactions, and take them to heart.

The prior two pillars are more cut and dry. *Here's how we create a vision. This is how we maintain clarity across the workplace.* Our third pillar isn't as simple, as it caters more to the intricacies of the human spirit. We have to recognize when something is needed, even when it is not requested verbally. We have to see when the support we are giving is not enough. Sometimes, it must be up to our intuition and discretion to recognize when a new form of support is needed. Other times, our commitment to open dialogue and employee empowerment will prove enough for them to approach us with new ideas. Either way, we can't sit idly by. It's our duty to provide.

At the surface, support relies on these three steps:

1) Discovery - find out what's needed

2) Follow-through - provide that support

3) Follow-up - check back to make sure it's enough

When young leaders take on a new job, I tell them, up front, I expect them to make mistakes and experience bumps along the road. They're trying to do their best job using their intuition and prior experiences. The mistakes they'll inevitably make will confirm they're on the right track, and they are! I want them to learn how to catch those mistakes, how to remove themselves from situations before it gets emotional, and how to take the time to reflect and adjust how they'll proceed in the future. I encourage them to talk to others on the leadership team, to apologize when needed, and to admit when they're wrong. These are expectations I like to set from the beginning, yet we can only expect employees to act accordingly when we provide an environment where they feel they have the support system to back them up. Rather than simply finding themselves in trouble, they have others around them to help them learn and improve.

In those moments of introspection, they can ask,

"What were my thoughts while the incident was occurring?"

"What got me here?"

"How will I do things differently?"

The goal is self-discovery and understanding why things went wrong. It's an accelerant to people becoming better employees and better leaders. You'll see your employees stretching themselves further than they ever did before.

AN EM'POWER'ED TEAM

You can tell it's working when you see a cohesive team—when you have a workforce of people with varying titles and authorities who all feel empowered. They step up, they trust their gut, and they make calls with full confidence. The only way to be a great decision-maker is to make a lot of decisions, and it's up to leadership to create the atmosphere for this to happen. Excellent support manifests itself into the employees, their actions, their confidence. You'll see it in the way they make decisions. Even in situations where they don't have the answer, they own that, and they seek to find out. Excellent support brings us back to the main focus, improving growth and development, providing clarity in the workplace, and strengthening the commitment to the company vision.

So Close, Yet So Far

You can have vision and clarity, but without support, you have a problem.

I was recently at an establishment that makes health smoothies. Their entire cash register system went down in the middle of my transaction. People behind me were waiting, ready to order. In the moment, they were trying to figure out what to do. Apparently, it's a common problem with these systems, and the owner's lack of upkeep, technology-wise, wasn't helping avoid problems.

What were they going to do?

They started handing out free smoothie cards as a way to show they were sorry. Unfortunately, I wanted the smoothie, not a card. I sensed something odd, and asked if they were capable of making the smoothies. They admitted they weren't. While they had a few basic recipes memorized, they didn't know the others without being able to reference the main system. In the moment, they were *wanting* to give customers free smoothies for their trouble, but because they didn't have the information needed to physically make the correct recipes, they could not. The support they needed, a book or menu to keep them on track, was missing.

So the system was down, the general manager (the only one with knowledge of all the recipes) wasn't present, and there was no other backup reference. This team had no way of producing a quality product for ready customers.

Furthermore, they had no way of taking a payment. In fact, they'd participated in community events before and had the necessary gadgets, like Square, but they didn't keep them in the store. The support they needed was so close, yet unavailable to them in the moment they needed it most.

There's support in the way a team *wants* to be supported, and there's support in the sense of, "If you need something, call me." The latter wasn't going to help them. What they needed was a backup in place and the knowledge of protocol when the main system was down.

If this store's leader had asked their team what they needed, or if they'd run them through scenarios of what could go wrong, they could have prevented this uncomfortable situation. With a strategy in place, a business runs smoothly. Customers wouldn't even know when things were different. What was lacking for my smoothie joint was the culture of support. Employees knew the vision. They wanted to make customers happy. They had an idea of what they needed to do.

Unfortunately, support was not in place to do so effectively.

Don't let this happen in your company.

Vision.

Clarity.

Support.

If any of the three are missing, the entire structure crumbles.

You've made it this far into *The 3 Pillars* for a reason and, hopefully, you're already taking action to implement and ensure Vision, Clarity, and Support are established and running strong in your workplace.

Making the Connection

Connection. Trust. If we can't connect with our team—taking the time to understand and value the things they do, talking about what's important to them—we can't create a thriving workplace. I have employees passionately involved in our community and it's a privilege to provide them with resources that help further their cause and help spread the word. Simple encouragement can help strengthen the rapport of the entire team.

One employee was starting a YouTube channel and wanted my approval. Not only was it okay, I wanted to see it. He shared it with me, and I look forward to following up on it and seeing how his current job provides content for his personal brand. By helping him connect the dots back to his role on my team, the bond becomes stronger. Everyone has a story and my personal goal is to encourage them to go off and do their thing—I'll even help when I can—but they must remember what's right in front of them. That employee may not do much with his YouTube channel, but even as a short-term hobby, he'll improve his ability to communicate and engage others. I get to help him stretch himself, try new things, reach a goal. That's a job well done. Many of today's leaders miss this. They don't understand the need to try these new things and to be inspired. That's where connection, or the lack thereof, becomes the main issue. "Tell me about yourself" is no longer sufficient. We must establish that connection, and with connection comes trust.

What I notice most when I look at the demographics of my team (and I bet you'll see this, as well), is there's a lot going on outside of work. They're graduating from school, moving out on their own, getting engaged, married, buying houses and cars, starting families, and the list goes on. They're experiencing real life, and to be supported and encouraged through these major milestones makes a wealth of difference. We have the opportunity to provide perspective and celebrate their successes. In places that don't share a common vision or focus on connection, these moments are easily missed. The same goes for the negatives: setbacks, illnesses, deaths. We can focus solely on the work at hand or we can be a shoulder to cry on. Which do you think will create a stronger bond within the team?

A DIFFICULT SHIFT

Who are you? Who's this person with this confidence to share analogies for days, providing people with direction and helping them connect the dots? It can be an out-of-body experience, at times. And that's exactly what it's like to grow as a leader. It's a continuous transition and each time you're given an opportunity to change, it's a chance to hit the reset button and make things even greater. People only know you by who you are today and how you do things today. The difficult part in these shifts is that we won't always get it right.

I'm very connected to the people who work for me. In my earlier days of leadership, that also meant I was overprotective. I'd seek out the smallest improvements and celebrate those rather than pushing for greatness. The celebration needed to wait until we'd exceeded the needs of the job. It wasn't until we were on the brink of failure that reality set in. I was letting my team down by accepting the bare minimum. Together, we had to reform expectations and challenge ourselves to be a better team.

Even now, my most significant challenge is how responsible I am for the development of my employees. What I do every day, what I role model, how I provide feedback and encouragement, is completely impacting their lives. As I've gotten older and more experienced in the leadership role, I've felt an even greater obligation to be sure nobody feels like just a cog in the system. They must know they're cared for and, through my actions, they must know I want them to succeed professionally and personally.

When you have large teams, it's easy to focus on the top performers, the hardest workers, and those who are completely committed. Then you have the other side of the spectrum—the ones who don't meet expectations and aren't engaged in the work. These two groups can take away your focus from the third, often invisible middle ground—the employees who do the necessary work, don't cause problems, but are the ones who are well aware they can work anywhere, under any leader. I want them to choose me.

Have I done enough?

Have I made an impact on them?

What are they gaining by being here?

I'll be the first to admit that knowing the effect I have on the lives of my team can be eye-opening and sometimes overwhelming. In the decades I've been doing this, my main, underlying thought pushing me to be a quality leader has been, "Don't let them down."

We have so many people counting on us so it's up to us to do better. We'll make mistakes but we'll be there to see them through. We'll help everyone be stronger employees and more successful people. The reason we have leaders is to provide support day-to-day and, essentially, that's why Vision, Clarity, and Support need to come to life.

FINAL WORDS

When it all comes down to it, be the leader you want. Trust your gut and do what's right. The hardest part of this work is reflecting on ourselves. We look in the mirror and ask, "Am I the leader for whom *I'd* want to work?"

Do my behaviors reflect the best in me?

Do I understand not everyone is motivated by the same things I am?

Most people in leadership roles got there through building relationships with their peers and inspiring others to get work done. Sure, some have made it into the role using aggression and verbal abuse, but that's not leadership. It's merely a job with a title, and very few people will fully engage while working for a person like that. We all recognize what we need from people is the best of themselves. When the work environment is negative, employees feel like they're just a cog in the system. They stop challenging themselves. Innovation comes to a halt. They'll do the bare minimum of what needs to be done until the day comes that they leave.

Take care of your people. As you consider the pieces you've read and how The 3 Pillars can come to life in your workplace, there will be some short-term pain as you think about your own setbacks, collect feedback from others, and come to realizations that maybe you were doing things you now consider to be wrong. It's time for that hard work to begin. This transition is an obstacle you must—*and can*—overcome. Passionate, great leaders must dig deep to surface their humility and use it to discover why disconnects exist and how they can be eliminated to build, or rebuild, your team.

If you've come to recognize...

- Your focus has been too much on numbers and revenue...

- You don't like how you've been communicating with your team...
- You keep losing your best people...
- You aren't the leader you thought you were...

...Then it's time to get to work. Right now.

Be happy when vision is misaligned or things aren't clear to your team. Be happy when they say they don't feel supported or empowered, because now you have a starting point. Now, you can address these issues head-on. Have honest conversations with your employees. Apologize. Then make a game plan. Real leadership is being comfortable in uncomfortable situations. Now that we've defined and owned the wound, we have the opportunity to heal it.

Redefine and restate the vision. Bring clarity into that vision and be sure everyone's expectations are clear. Then provide the right environment to support the vision and the team. Growth and improvement flow through all three pillars and, with time, things will all turn around. You'll be able to proudly boast,

"I AM the leader I'd want to work for."

COMING FROM EXPERIENCE

My mom was seventeen when she had me and nineteen when she had my sister. Throughout the majority of my childhood, she was a single mom raising two kids and working multiple part-time jobs while putting herself through school. I remember going to work with her, being dropped off at the school's daycare, and being helped by other families. Once she remarried, we moved often. I'm talking, every four years. In fact, the longest I ever lived in one city was during college—five years, and even then I moved four times. My first real job was at my uncle's catering business. I was a dish washer. It was labor intensive, but it allowed me to buy my own shoes. I also worked a paper route, and here's where I pushed my first experiences in customer service to the extreme. I'd meet my customers, ask where they preferred I leave their paper, and put the extra effort into making their experience unique. In return, Christmas would come around, and I'd find myself getting gifts and tips from these people. I prided myself in doing hard work. It's how money was made, and I quickly learned the benefits of having a positive relationship with every customer.

One year, my summer job was working at McDonald's. The next year, it was McDonald's and Rite Aid. I wanted a paycheck. I wanted to show my family I was willing to take initiative and work hard. I felt this sense of responsibility to the general public and took my experiences working for my uncle and my paper route and applied them to each new role. The burgers had to be made perfect. The workspace had to be immaculate. The customers had to have a good time. I had extra coupons at the ready. I joked with the older ladies about needing to see their ID to buy alcohol when they were very clearly old enough to purchase it legally. I had fun with it and it took all of one day at Rite Aid to earn my first raise. Little did I know, my high school experiences, my interest in serving the public, and my willingness to accept new responsibilities—learning everything that went with them—were the early seeds planted in my lifelong pursuit of being a quality leader.

MY JOURNEY TO LEADERSHIP

I just turned forty. That's a milestone in itself. With that comes more than twenty years of retail experience, and I've easily spent three-quarters of that time in leadership roles. My very first role in leadership, though I didn't hold an official title, was at a small mom and pop music store in Kalamazoo, Michigan called Music Galaxy. While working there, I was deejaying at local clubs and doing college radio. I had limited knowledge of the music industry but, nevertheless, I was tasked with building the music production section of the retail store, bringing in the knowledge and resources needed to support the local community. My career aspirations were in the music industry, and this mix of jobs—deejaying, radio, and retail—brought everything together. They introduced me to the concepts I emphasize today about connection and meaning in the workplace, no matter the role, no matter the employee.

But more on that later.

After college, I moved to California and got a job at the retail mecca of music production—Guitar Center. There, I worked as a guitar salesperson, and I happened to be good at it. Only, I didn't play guitar. When an opportunity to be the Pro Audio Manager showed up, I quickly snatched it. Now was the time to learn the good, the bad, and the ugly of my field. I was now a salaried employee, working long hours, and leading a commissioned team who each held their own specialties but didn't necessarily work together. I brought in different vendors to customize the training, and we grew the business. Unfortunately, the fantastic general manager we started with soon left, and he was replaced by someone who only cared about numbers. He was unreliable, all over the place, and ended up having sexual harassment charges filed against him. A lot happened in the short nine months I was there. That's it. Nine months. I had an exceptional team and enjoyed the challenges that came with my role, but I also got a crash course in company politics, integrity (or lack thereof), and what happens when you're the one the employees turn to. I'm the one who handled HR when my female employee came to me about our GM's behavior, and I'm the one who felt a responsibility to my team when this knowledge came to light. The outcome, to me, was unacceptable, and I knew I couldn't function in a place like that.

WHEN BIG CHANGES LEAD TO BIG RESULTS

The next phase of my journey brought me to Best Buy, from which came a decade of leadership growth in a variety of roles and locations. I began there part-time in the audio department, but they quickly decided they wanted me full-time. I was hesitant. At the time, I was opening a music studio in Los Angeles with some friends, and I liked my Best Buy job as it was—easy, fun, little responsibility. I resisted the move to full-time. Management pushed harder. I relented. Now, I was in charge of the employee satisfaction team, then senior of a department, and, finally, when my general manager was asked to move to another store that needed help, he insisted on me transferring as well. Again, here I was kicking and screaming. I didn't want to move from my store—a simple one mile from my house—to one that was unfamiliar and twenty-two miles of L.A. traffic away. This particular GM, Don, inspired me with his leadership style, though, so I went and became the supervisor of the audio department. The reset button was hit, and I got to take over a team, helping them improve and align with the company's expectations. We were a two-man show, Don and I. He worked directly with the leaders setting the expectations, and I worked on the floor ensuring those expectations were a reality. Then I went on a vacation. When I returned, Don was no longer our GM, and I learned our store had been selected for a top-secret project. Corporate was seeking a new leader, someone who could innovate and empower, rather than focus on the standards. They brought in Gil.

Gil turned out to be a great mentor of mine. His first day, he introduced himself and said, "Someone in this room will be a better general manager than me in the future. My job is to find out who you are and help you get there."

His humility mixed with empowerment made a huge impact not just on me, but on the entire team. As wonderful as Don had been, I was excited for the changes that would come. Don was dedicated to his people as a reflection of his leadership role. With Gil, it was his life's work. The next few weeks brought new learning opportunities, for both my new leader and myself. One day, Gil pulled me into his office with concerns.

"I need to understand something. I've spoken with everyone in this building, and nobody has any constructive criticism to offer about how you lead and who you are as a team member. I need to know why."

For the first time, I got to fully explain my philosophies — the earliest seeds of *The 3 Pillars*. Every team member needed to *feel* it was a team, that there was a bigger picture, and that they were doing their job for a reason. There had to be purpose. And there had to be open communication. I explained it was all about development. For the most part, people want to do good work, and when they aren't succeeding it means they need training, help, perspective...conversation. It's up to the leaders to give it to them. I told Gil my backstory and he offered me a new job. He didn't know what this job was—he couldn't know—and he couldn't tell me anything more about it unless I accepted the promotion. At the time, I was still adjusting to working at the location without my former partner in leadership. I'd only moved there because I'd known Don and I could do great things. Now, here I was, having to commit to a blind job under a leader I was still getting to know.

"I can't be like Don, no. But if you want to learn, develop, and grow in your career, I'm the guy for you."

We shook hands. It was a deal.

Then I was flown out to DC for two weeks. My flight was booked as fast as that handshake was over.

One day, I was Mr. Hip Hop in my Nikes and camouflage. The next, I was business casual in Washington, training to roll out a new company-wide philosophy. Things seemed to fast forward from there. Training, traveling, transitioning from stores to behind-the-scenes amongst consultants and training teams. I saw new store cultures develop; witnessed leaders succeed, stumble, and overcome obstacles; and experienced stores all over the country.

From one coast to the other, I found myself in the Southeast U.S., and then I took my biggest leap. I built a house in Jacksonville, Florida and made a transition from ten successful years with Best Buy to day one with Apple, Inc.

I'm in my tenth role of, in my opinion, being the person who is ultimately accountable for the results, development, and experience of individual stores. It's a career filled with mistakes, new lessons and constant change. I work in service of my employees and of The 3 Pillars—vision, clarity and support. These are the essential tools needed to ensure your employees can be their best. This book is your friendly operation manual.

RINSE AND REPEAT

The work won't be done once you've established The 3 Pillars in your workplace. There will be times when you experience a bad quarter, you're struggling to meet a budget, or your own direct leaders don't think you're meeting expectations. These old wounds seem to resurface, but we can stop, recommit, and consider the actions we need to take next.

THE LEADER NEEDS A LEADER, TOO.

When we consider The 3 Pillars, we must also look upward. Are we getting a clear, aligned vision from our own leaders? Are our roles and expectations clear? Have we clarified what we need from them? Is the support there? Do we know what resources are available to us, and are we using them?

Take on the challenge of creating the world you want. Are you working in an environment that allows you to be your best self? And if that environment can't be built and maintained, then consider the hardest question of all: Is it the right place for you? Or are there other industries or jobs where you can more easily be the leader you want to be? It takes a lot of emotion, transparency, and discomfort, but by doing the right work, trusting your instincts, being a positive force, and truly caring about those you work with, you'll get through all these obstacles much quicker.

THESE 3 PILLARS ARE YOURS NOW.

You've reached the end of this crash course on The 3 Pillars of Success. If you haven't already, it's now time to take what you've learned and apply it to your own work environment. What changes can you make? How can you inspire and re-energize your team, shifting the focus to a unified vision?

There's always room for improvement, and it's never too late to start. As you become the leader you've always wanted to be, you'll inspire those among you to do the same. Imagine a new generation of workplaces where teams are empowered, aligned and connected, and where productivity is high, customers are happy, and turnover is low.

Now, make it happen.

Lorenzo Flores, a twenty year veteran in retail leadership, has rejuvenated, inspired, and rebuilt over a dozen companies and teams throughout his career. With a passion for music, MMA, and podcasting (check out *Hacking Your Leadership!*), he understands the importance of connecting personal vision to the workplace. Currently the Store Leader for a

major technology retailer in Orlando, FL—
and now author—Flores's insights, experiences, and philosophies on leadership excellence
are the fuel to ignite every leader's optimum
potential.

Acknowledgments

The completion of this book could not have been accomplished without the support, mentorship and guidance of my friend Jamie Blair. Thank you for collecting, challenging and organizing my crazy thoughts and persevering through this 3 year project.

Thanks to all of the friends and family that kept encouraging me and asking me how the book was coming along. Your words were the daggers of accountability that I needed to push through the finish line.

I would also like to thank the direct leaders, peers, mentors, and influencers that shaped my leadership platform and made me the leader I am today;

Christian Abrahamson, Chuck Admire, Brad Anderson, Megan Arcuri, Albert Austin, Shari Ballard, Gerrod Boykin, Amber Cales, Jeff Cox, Ramzi Daklouche, Toni David, Gil Dennis, Victoria Diaz, Bruce Dillion, Michael Donovan, Mickey Donovan, Beth Eifert, Derek Fender, Eric Gaffka, PJ Garcia, Julie Gilbert, Paula Goodman, Glen Hansen, Jeff Hicks, Farid Khansarinia, Dean Kimberly, Jennifer Lai-ahsang, Juan Lorenzo, Jason Loshelder, Steve Maxcy, Paul McKim, Omar Njie, Derek Palmer, Kal Patel, Edwin Rios, Joe Rogan, Nick Russo, Don Savage, Shawn Score, Jason Smith, Chris Stark, Jorge Suazo, Ben Um, Gary Vaynerchuk, Don Warshaw, Ryan Warshaw

I would also like to indirectly thank the few leaders that showed me what bad leadership looked like, as you also influenced me as much as those above.

Finally, to my caring, loving, and supportive wife, Courtney: my deepest gratitude. Your encouragement and patience was very much appreciated. This is for our beautiful daughters; Allora Elizabeth and Gabriella Marie.

#RiteAid   #MusicGalaxy   #GuitarCenter119
#BBY114   #BBY111   #WildWildWestminster
#BBY119 #BBY117 #T2TrainingDept #BBY507
#BBY435   #BBY515   #BBY430   #R111   #CFL
#MT3   #NorthFloridaFlagship   #MT2   #R291
#TEAMAltamonte   #HackingYourLeadership
#LifeOfLozo

LAUNCH TEAM

Kerri Stephenson, Doug Stephenson Jr., Alicia Flores, Charles "Chuck" Stephenson, John Stephenson, Chris Stark, Frankie Liz, Squiggy DiGiacomo, Christian Abrahamson, Sean Tibbetts, Jay Harvey, Robb Chamberlain, Chris Templo, Anthony James, Angelica Rosado-Rivera, Sean Amire, Sarah Hernandez, Randy Nathan, Vincent J Gates, Ryan T. Jaghab Esq., Leonard Harris, Lance Mitchell, Adam Penkunas, Elo Petrosian, Clay Hackett, Lance Robinson, Tracy Meyers, Damian B Wilson, Alan Kracht, John McNeil, Audrey Seiler, Keyshia Littleton, Tanya Stanton, Chris Cuffie, Charles Rollins, David W Gould, Michael C. Pittman IV, MaXi Jacobs, Jackie Plonka, Michelle Ross, Cindy Wilson, Betsy Brocker, Maurice Overton, Chris Gaffka, Andrew Marrocco, Abigail Hanna, Thomas Thurston, E-Man, Shaun Hayes, Jay Maragh, Chantel Ma, Dirah Bolden, Kenneth Gilmore, Ana Simmons, Nicole Bartolomeo, Charles Williams, Matt Ritter, Ishabah Wilder, Nicky Johnson, Ormal Ali, Craig Hurst, Gardell Branch Jr., Steven Carmichael, Benjamin Um, Rob Wodrich, Mike Faulkner, Craig Closson

Follow Lorenzo on Social Media

Lorenzo Flores on LinkedIn

@HackingYourLeadership on Instagram / Facebook / LinkedIn

@LeadershipMemes on Facebook / Twitter

@Life_Of_Lozo on Instagram

Life of Lozo on YouTube

@LifeOfLozo on Twitter

www.HackingYourLeadership.com

www.VisionClaritySupport.com

www.LifeOfLozo.com

Credits

Cover Art Design: Chris Stark and Kyle Willis

Artwork: Kyle Willis

Editors: Chris Stark & Nicole Bailey (Proof Before You Publish)

Photography: Courtney Flores

Wardrobe: Daniel Motorca (www.TheTailorShopInc.com)